Palewell Press

Tiger and Clay
Syria Fragments

Rana Abdul Fattah

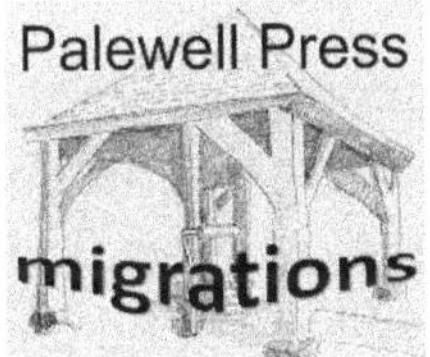

Tiger and Clay – Syria Fragments

Published by Palewell Press Ltd
http://www.palewellpress.co.uk/

First Edition

ISBN 978-0-995535-12-1

A CIP catalogue record for this title is available from the British Library.

Palewell Press Ltd supports the Forest Stewardship Council® (FSC®) the leading international forest-certification organisation. Our books carrying the FSC® label are printed on FSC®-certified paper. Their printing and binding complies with ISO 14001 (Environmental Management) and 50001 (Energy Management).

Dedication

To my parents and siblings, blood related and life related, hoping for a soon reunion. I dedicate my book to all the troubled Syrian souls alive and dead. I hope peace finds its way into our souls.

Acknowledgements

This book would not have been possible without the help of many people. I thank Juan delGado for giving Camilla Reeve some of my writings. If not for his faith in my writing, I wonder if I would have thought of putting the manuscript together for publication. I thank Palwasha Mirbacha for reading and commenting on an early draft. Her enthusiasm and dedication in the task was humbling. I would also like to thank Abdullah al-Riyami for his sensitive editing of the text; he preserved my voice. I thank Akshi Singh for her meticulous reading of the text and comments. To all of them I owe an immense gratitude in giving me the confidence to let go of the text. I also thank Souad Osseiran for her insights and editing of the book, and her help during the process to prepare the manuscript for publication.

I thank countless people who inspired different parts of the book. They will remain unnamed.

As always, my deepest thanks and gratitude goes to my family for their patience, support and faith in me over the years. To my sisters who were kind enough to take the time to read my first poems when I was a teenager; you nurtured me and gave me the confidence to keep writing. To my brother, yoldaşım, as they say in Turkish, as we are two peas in a pod.

Tiger and Clay

Syria Fragments

As you smile across from me while few steps separate us from the hello-hug and kisses; the war and oppressed memory, the anxious rebelling self, evaporate like meaningless strangers. I smile back at your face. I feel happy, utterly happy. An effortless happiness encircles me. Have you ever felt the wet ground after rain when your bus stops for a break on a road to Amasya[1]? Have you ever felt your face chill as you go down from the bus to smell the ground? It is the breakage of things, the interruption of time, of possibility. The happiness of being in love before accumulations of time and memory. A raw wet ground on the margin of time.

The seeds are left by the garbage on the coastline of Samatya. These seeds are made in Syria. That much I remember, that much I don't want to forget. Samatya or Psamatheia is an old neighbourhood in İstanbul on the beautiful Marmara Sea. The name is Greek and means sandy. It was inhabited by Greeks and Armenians, and now by Turks, Armenians, Kurds and yes, the Syrians who brought their seeds here. The seeds are a snack we used to take on sayran. Sayran is a

---

[1] Amasya is a city in northern Turkey in the Black Sea region.

Turkish word meaning a picnic. The Armenians received Syrians well here as far as I know and have experienced it myself with my landlord. Perhaps they have not forgotten their experience. My landlord who is Armenian has been very good to me.

Every time I go to the coast, I see my folks. It was not this way two years ago.

"You should not live like a migrant!" I tell him angrily. "You should move and go out to the world and work and live." But what does it mean to live like a migrant? It is the stillness that I meant; the uncertainty, the routine, the lack of movement. They are taking their seeds to the coast and hence moving; living.

"If you want to live like a migrant, go live with the guys down the street. I do not want to live like a migrant." This conversation took place and it seems we both agreed to what living like a migrant meant. We did not say what it meant, but we both knew. If you don't live like a migrant, you will be called one. That should not make any difference to you, because who knows, fifty years down the line, other migrants will come to Samatya and you will receive them as the lawful inhabitant of the neighbourhood. Thus, time always has the upper hand over movement. You have to move to stop living like a migrant.

Because movement will give your waiting a meaning.

Mary, my landlord, came to visit at Eid. She brought Turkish sweets, baklawa, with her. We do not visit each other much, but we love each other. I have been living in her apartment for almost 5 years. We talked about her tired mother who lives in Bakırköy and about her sister who passed away. I asked her about her siblings and why they do not attend to their mother. She said they have been living in Europe for ages and they only come here for short visits, so she has to take care of her mother. She told me why they migrated to Europe. In September in the 50s, they attacked Armenians and Greeks in this neighbourhood, she said. Most of her family and the people she knew fled to other parts of the world. As she described how they were attacked, her heart raced and she started crying.

"I become very emotional when I talk about this," she said.

I stopped asking. I wanted to know how it felt to be unwanted, and how she fought back to remain. I guess I have the answer. Living in this country for 6 years and without papers for the last two, I am fighting for my right to remain in the country I want to be in. It is not easy to live without papers, or, as a lawyer in an NGO for refugee rights called me, an irregular resident. She scared the hell out of me as she told me the only solution to become legal is to leave the country with the risk I might be banned from entering again for 5 years. She was lovely and very helpful. I can be a lawyer myself knowing the law regarding my foreignness.

A good friend of mine once told me that the only true things are the things you hold onto in your mind as you move on. Your childhood is not true, but what you hold of it in your thoughts is true. Don't you think it's wonderful that you treasure your truths? You have the real thing and will always have it. I am legal and a person no matter what my passport is, or lawyers or states think of me. Fair enough! I have the right to be wherever I want to.

we are people who are believed to make love in
silence,
we are people who are believed to cry in silence.
we are people who are believed to live in silence;
we are people who are being killed in silence.
but when we rise up, we bring up all the noise;
and you might want to record it,
because our noise is a valuable symphony,
whereas yours is parasitical discord!

Every time people get frustrated with their states, they project their hate and frustration onto migrants and refugees or whatever they call them these days. Turks think Syrians are living better in Turkey than they are, that they have more than Turks, and the Turkish state is giving them more than its own. The reality is quite different as usual. The media and state propaganda always tell half the story.

Once again, we are the problem. I am so tired of trying to understand humans; so tired of trying to cope with having to wear the refugee name in this country. It is not like it is different anywhere else. Here, to be racist against a foreigner is considered socially natural, meaning they do not blink even if they know you very well. It is the effect of the puritan version of nationalism that was enforced on this country following the fall of the Ottoman empire.

We stand in line to pay the bills. A woman expresses her anger at the AKP[2] party and at voters. A woman behind me, encouraged by the angry woman in front of me, adds Syrians voted for AKP, and they talk to each other while other women in line roll their eyes trying to ignore the political conversation. It seems to me like a little

---

[2] Justice and Development party.

bill-payment parliament, then I started getting overwhelmed by my socially anxious self. Stay put, I told my anxious self, you have the right to be here. I stood firm until my refugeeness - weak, vulnerable, burden, crisis, political card, herd of sheep filled into death boats from Turkey to be returned from Europe, trade of humans by smugglers and states - creeped all over into my head, and I left the tense place.

I know we are survivors and fighters, but the images and concepts in the media and political discourse about refugees sneak into our consciousness until we believe it to be true and we start embracing these images and concepts unconsciously.

I remembered a childhood memory from my geography class back in Syria. We had a lesson about migration in ancient times. People used to migrate at times of drought, moving to other places for food and water; no image of migrants back then creeped up my head; it read so naturally. Now, they are so creative with images and concepts of migrants and asylum seekers that you become so full, you do not know where to start your mental cleansing process to preserve your human face.

"We will talk about stereotyping today and I will give you an example to understand the word. As a Turkish person, I have seen many Syrian beggars in Istanbul and so I say all Syrians are beggars. This is a stereotype. Do you understand the concept now?" said a Turkish teacher to her students in an institution for teaching Turkish to foreigners. The class is all Syrian students who were awarded a scholarship to learn Turkish in preparation to enter higher education in Turkey.

The teacher's provocative statement initiated different responses from the students. What is the problem exactly for a teacher who speaks three languages, exposed to three cultures, to feel so comfortable in deliberately and invoking such an image and concept of Syrians before a Syrian audience?

There are many efforts to deconstruct the term "refugee." The whole system built around this term needs deconstruction be it - thriving NGOs or asylum regimes. Here is my definition of what being a refugee is, you are a slave waiting for someone or some state to give you rights and make you so happy with what is given; a good example here is Turkey and Syrians' feverous ecstasy with the Turkish state.

Syrians migrating to Europe will not stop because of an enslaving deal between different states buying and selling human lives in exchange for privileges. At the same time, they do not stop milking the presence of refugees all over the world. Weapons sold to keep the war going, NGOs starting projects to launder money, jobs revitalizing the economies of Syria's neighbours, but these do not count. You are a refugee, be happy with what we give, but please let us keep milking you as you are such a revitalizing force for the economy.

I am so happy migrating birds and animals do not have visa issues and fences in the sky to halt their efforts to survive, but humans with their mindful consciousness do actually build walls around themselves.

Academic and researcher Ourooba Shetewi wrote on her Facebook page,

I keep reading about refugees; good-hearted posts and articles and others truly depressing and bad... but what both seem to fail to realize is that refugees are essentially human beings... as simple as that! It is not surprising that mean-spirited pieces dehumanize refugees, but it is disheartening when good-spirited pieces also fall into the trap. They fish for good stories as if to prove a point! They present those stories as extraordinary human acts when they simply are human stories of regular human beings!

Refugees are people with all their contradictions; good and bad. They had their lives in their countries before they were forced to be refugees, but they are still pretty much the same people.

Stop treating them as if they are aliens!

I have been a refugee my whole life! I was born a refugee like my parents before me and I passed it on to my children! We are basically refugees for life for a variety of political reasons we had nothing to do with, but that is another story for another day.

But practically, I was just another resident in Syria with my own individual story; dreams, difficulties and all the mundane things that make us human. I lived my life regardless and despite of the term refugee. It actually seemed to matter more for others than it mattered for me! It only mattered for me where it was relevant, but it seemed to matter in every tiny little aspect for other people once they heard the magic word and I was left to feel like an alien and trying to explain or just eventually giving up!

So try to remember the very basic and essential truth about refugees; we are people. Plain and simple...

I saw my face in the mirror,
and all I can see is your face.
I look into my eyes,
realize
despise
the hardship of this time.
Still I recognize,
I acknowledge
the face in the back of my mind,
but there is no way
I could see my face in the mirror
from the back of my mind.

I sigh
Cry
and your face is mocking mine.

Drink with me the nectar of absence,
And cheers! we are pseudo-humans.

It is not one of the good days. Good as in normal. It is one of those days where you go blank and lost. You start dancing in front of the mirror, changing one or two outfits. You look at the mirror and you adore yourself. I am adorable and I am enjoying every bit and piece of the dancing Me in front of the mirror. I feel my ego growing higher than my stature and fatter than my waist. It holds me up there on my feet and I jump over the floor intoxicated with the love of myself. I am so in love of myself while dancing in front of the mirror in this blank day. My mind is off and the phone keeps ringing. People in the middle of this huge city are demanding some sort of help. Yes, damn it! Why do I have to pick up the phone and mutter to them excuses they know are not true. Sorry I was asleep when you called. I am very skilled with social apologies that I don't give a fuck whether they believe me or not. I haven't been doing my own stuff, and I am very narcissistic. Do you get it? No, keep calling and I will be asleep.

"Hello, do you know of any place that we could rent in your area, a family is coming from your hometown and they are looking for a place."

Yes, well I am very narcissistic! it is my hometown so should I feel obliged? No, well, I will look for a place and get back to you. You know I won't! They invite me for dinner, and because it is an off day, I plan to go at 7 p.m. I wear my jumper and take off in the rain.

I pull over with my mighty legs to the shop at the corner and ask for birthday candles. I don't know whether she is 3 years old or more. So let me get 5 candles I tell myself. I go off from the shop empty-handed. A man standing next to me with a cigarette which was about to burn my beautiful jacket that I happily bought, something which does not happen very often: to happily buy stuff. Anyways, I give him the look, produce the social pardon and get back on track to the pasta[3] shop. I window-shop for a good 5 minutes and go in hurriedly to buy luxurious pasta, the gift for the 3 or more years old child to make her happy because she likes to have birthdays on a weekly basis.

I catch the bus, place my good self next to the window and start observing the people on the bus by their reflection. Two women are sitting across from me. They must be smartly thinking, "oh she has a pasta and she is going to surprise someone, a friend, a lover." I know it is just because I am holding this bag that they would be inventing scenarios revolving around the pasta

---

[3] Pasta is cake in Turkish

bag. Can't you just see a bag without making the effort to fantasize a story of the bag of a stranger on the bus? Yes, I know. There is nothing else to do when you're on a bus and we need to amuse ourselves. It is one mental entertainment. I have another scenario in mind. I was trying to decide where to stop and which stop is closer to their place. I have tried many stops before, and I have been living in the city for almost two years, but I still cannot make good sense of directions. I love stability when it comes to places, that I would rather stop at the same stop so it becomes familiar.

We are all strangers on the road and I can easily define the language of the strangers on the road. But why do I care to even enjoy deducing the language of those strangers while carrying pasta in this blank day. Yes, it seems like an existential drama that I am making up to make up for the blankness of today.

It is rainy and warm. The reddish tiled streets suck the water of heaven in a mix of the man-made will to grow feet and the divine will to grow life.

I walk and the grey tiled streets ache,
There is no language and codes to define our encounters.
Transparent as if there is no social or physical gravity!
The stiff cement softens my feet, embraces my steps, urges me to walk!

Walking, it sucks burdens out of my shoes,
Sucks heaviness out of my feet!
Stretches endless ahead of me
Like some intimate silent lover!

I am willing to spend a good evening with a family who escaped the war in Syria. Here we go, I call on the man to open the door for me, and I sit on the few stairs at the building gate, waiting to be welcomed in. The man is not there and they cannot open the gate. I wait for a few minutes, conjure my silent companion and I bring it close to my mouth to light it up. We shine together for a cat to notice and seek us out along with two bags of garbage and the well-rested pasta at my side. "You must be full of bugs, but you are such a beautiful bundle of dirt, seeking attention and food. I had a cat in my apartment for a couple of months and she killed me with bugs, so I kicked her ass out. I had to read for hours about flea life cycles and trying all kind of treatments for the sick furniture at home," I tell the dirty cat.

Finally, a little handsome boy of 10 opens the gate to their small refuge here in the centre of the large city, Istanbul. I am very hungry; I did not have breakfast and it is almost 8 in the evening, and all I am thinking of is when they are going to put out the food so I can enjoy a home-made Syrian meal. The family setting can make my appetite easily swell, something which does not happen very often.

The feast is spread and I am fluttering around it like a butterfly waiting to be initiated into the fire, however, I know the minute I start feasting I will remember something and it will ruin the initiation ritual of the familiar food. Along with the spinach and potato pies, beans and rice, and Fatosh[4] comes the fire. It is neither the fire of the tiger nor the fire of the appetite. It is just the fire of initiation which kills the butterfly while having the meal.

I break up the social grammar again; I cannot hold myself back from starting the initiation. I rush into the potato pies because I do not trust my appetite, it might stop midway and I might not be able to enjoy such a familiar feast again anytime soon. Lilian, with all the peace and forgetfulness that is absent from my interior, sits beside me with her little feet and little hands on the floor ready to mess up the food.

Hasan, her father, tells me how she can understand everything. Three days ago, they shelled the city and she was telling her father how her uncle must have become a martyr and she started crying. I still want to believe she has peace and forgetfulness. I do want to believe. It is too early for her to be initiated in the fire!

I need to leave and catch the bus, so let us have the weekly birthday of Lilian. The pasta is

---

[4] A type of salad.

waiting for us to happily devour it. The family starts singing, "happy birthday to you..." I interrupt them singing the same song in Arabic, "sana helwa ya gamil...sana helwa ya gamil...sana helwa ya lilian." It is very easy to lead the crowd, isn't it? Well, it was easy to get them to change the birthday song from English to Arabic. I mean do we really have to celebrate our birthdays with the sounds of another tongue from another place, context, and time.

Damn it!

I am schizophrenic!

English is easier to write in. I do not have to carry my legacy, consciousness, tree, divinity while typing. I still do not understand why I cannot write in my mother tongue. I give myself a lot of excuses, but it seems that I just do not have the guts to venture myself in its heavily-loaded context. It is not risky to be in another language, is it? Perhaps it is a way to counter linguistic hegemony. I am from Syria and I write in English. So I place my good self in your hegemonic language. Fair enough!

I am schizophrenic!

Unlock this language in our knotted fingers,
Decode the nervous feeling in my ears, the fine sounds unheard before.
There is so much in us for the grammar to systematize.
There is a wild chaos in the dawn utterance, a delicious fear of being silent with you lest you understand the language I have never mastered.
Forget our holy language and let us converse in its interpretations.
We are just too human, two humans.

4 a.m. in Istanbul. I have tried to sleep three times. I got up, ate a baklava, made a coffee with cardamom. I am loaded, and I don't think I will get unloaded anytime soon. My interior is so full of shit that smells like rotten food. It has been kept in for a long time. Time, yes. The more time passes, the more I keep in food, and I cannot get it out!

We are made of clay; we are made to survive! Those who commit suicide are the ones who cannot handle their clay!

I love you! I need to go protest in solidarity with Egyptian women. There will be an international sit-in, and I will go with the women of Amargı[5] organization. Other people will join too. We will protest in front of the Egyptian Embassy in Bebek.

Sabrin sınırı var!

Sabrın sınırı var!

Patience has limits! Yes, it has. I have always hated activism since the time I was introduced to it by my activist ex. Being all over the Palestinian cause and freedom, and pressuring me to be an activist. I was somewhere else. I didn't want to be one. At the time, I thought it was just a way to diverge from the Syrian reality. You fight for

---

[5] Former women organization in Turkey.

Palestinian freedom, and the problem is that you yourself are not free! Activism is another class of bourgeois who speak English, attend conferences, travel around, and speak on behalf of the people. How can I, in the name of the people, speak on their behalf? What makes my voice more audible? English, privilege, you name it! What is more fashionable and appealing to the western media and the west and western-like audiences.

We are a group of hungry women in Taksim waiting to get on the bus. We rush into the bus and start the journey. Istanbul traffic makes you wonder: How beautiful Istanbul traffic is when you are sitting beside the window in the bus reflecting on all that was and all that can be, but not all that is!

The present is a bunch of women chanting for Arab women. I chant, "The women of Egypt are not alone!" I should have written something like on the behalf of women of Syria, but that would make me an activist. It is funny! I am the only veiled woman in the crowd which makes me very photogenic. This is the unsolved dilemma for the great minds of activists. There is a set of political values you need to uphold, force on yourself to become part of this group. Hijab is not one of them. The hijab in most of these groups makes you photogenic and strong when only in such a context.

My mother finished her primary school education and she married young. She raised a beautiful strong family and they call her "a house wife". You cannot fight for anyone. There is no victim. You can neither fight for me nor for my mother. The clay knows best how to handle its nature.

Get out from your cocoons and call a woman a human being. It can only start when a woman becomes a human being and a man becomes a human being.

I have always believed that it's within the household. Parents can raise human beings instead of raising up women and men. This might be too much to handle within the patriarchal mountain in all the societies, and Egypt is no exception. I was not raised in a household with the pink and blue dilemma. I have experienced patriarchy at home though, but in a different manner, as layers, the surrounding society forcing it on the unit and not vice versa.

I chart my way through the crowd,
and I know how hollow.
these figures make me feel.
I look for more cucumber to chop my nervousness.
And look for more carrots to chop my alienation.

I don't want to be here. Never wanted to be here.
Never wanted to be anywhere.
These steps I have taken!
These faces I make familiar.
These streets I didn't want to walk.
These words I never wanted to utter and the words I
didn't want to hear.

About to faint amongst the fine-cultured elite,
who publish knowledge, convene conferences and
commence change!
I want to eat more cucumber!
Give me more carrots, caffeine doesn't numb my
nerves!

I go for a smoke to put myself together and suddenly
there is a Turkish bath,
several beautiful women moving gracefully.
There is a woman who bends her back gracefully and
whispers
something in the ears of a man. Only one man
surrounded by beautiful women!
I step ahead, could this be heaven!
And these are the man's nymphs!

Or is it the Turkish era!
I must be fainting or are there modern sultans?
I better chop more cucumber!

In the reverie of our private sphere, eternity is the only time zone. Past, present and future rest on your soft tight body irrelevant and at peace. It is a motionless resurrection, and the release is just another charge for more eternities.

Let me wear you and have my times at hold. I map the curves of your neck, grab your hands, kiss your fairly big mouth and closed eyes. Drive you up the wall, and I wear you!

I do my ablution and pray, “God, thank You for being the only one who can embrace me!”

In the clay, there is a tiger and the problem is neither in the question nor is in the text, it is in interpretation. You can listen or read the answer in folk literature and Sufi music. To belong is to have a grammar and in grammar there are exceptions. You can never belong fully except to the gravity of the universe. We belong anyways.

Peace.

We can only appreciate peace through conflict. We can only know peace through conflict. We can only crave peace through conflict. Is it as simple as binary oppositions? Heaven/hell, love/hate, peace/conflict and so on. We call images names, the signifier/signified. Then, we associate words with different images, and even better we contextualize images. Yes, you can come up with your version of peace and spread it to the folk.

It is 3 in the afternoon and I have to go renew my resident permit in Istanbul. I am stupid when it comes to practical things, I cannot even remember how to turn on the hot water. I miss you, you keep on at me when it comes to practical things. However, I need to know them and try to remember the practical things every time. I take a quick shower, dress, dance a bit in front of the mirror and start off to get my legal stay in Istanbul.

To Emniyat, Yabancı Şube![6]

I love windows. We are foreigners even to the world.

---

[6]Immigration Management Directorate

Peace.

I know I could have finished the whole process if I had pushed the şube mudur[7] a bit more. It is funny that I procrastinate so much and then I want to get my thing done in one day. Damn it!

Syrians are familiar. I know them from their accent, looks, and dress. They, too, like me are getting their stay legal in Istanbul. They, too, like me are trying to be at peace. Get out of a warzone for some peace. We need to keep the Syrian kind.

Peace.

For a long time, mother was home, and she above all was my peace. I take off the necklace she gave me ten years ago. This is the second time. I take it off, swallow my choke and my tearful eyes. The first time, he wanted it off while we were making love. It was not serious. Now, I want my own peace. We are born alone, die alone, and we are resurrected alone.

---

[7] Branch manager

There comes a time for the lemon tree to blossom and smell
like heaven in the palm of my hands.
Restore my senses of yore!

Yes, there will be a time
when I will be back running in the backyard of our old house, and swing beside the olive tree in a hot afternoon when every one is taking lunch and I am singing while mother calls me to go inside.

Mother! The twinge awakens my dejected wretched heart,
my insensitive burgeoning singing.
I can't hear you! The tones blocked my ears, mother!

A light shines through lined-up lanterns
on both sides of the quiet street.
Sounds of high heels and men's coughs.
And here and there, is a restaurant or a bar.
Or a café offering coffee and drinks.
hearing my two friends' nonsense,
I climb over some ball- like stones.
I say, "my friend am I not a better statue of the famous one?"
And she says, "I will call you my sister then!"
I say, " I am your sister forever!"
We laugh and we walk further.

I tell her I am going to miss those streets soon,
I am going to miss my mother the most.
My mother who eases my silence,
my sadness, my loneliness.

I am going to miss her too,
there should be a vaccine against those feelings.
I envy people who objectify their feelings.
I walk further thinking one day I wouldn't be hurt for anything.
Thinking one day I will be immune.
Thinking that one day is the day I stop living.

I cannot possibly make you my home. You are subject to change like time and feelings. It is not a matter of fear of getting hurt or the possibility of dealing with your loss; it is rather the awareness of life's continuity within me regardless of any emotional or physical attachment, regardless of belonging. I am an intense human being, intense as in passion is my engine and it ignites my survival, and I am not yours or anyone else's because I simply cannot be.

You are beautiful like a palm tree with ripe grapes drooping all over. The multi-faceted beauty of yours switches between the nerdy suppressed self to the wilder, but at peace, nature. Your exquisite discreet layered brain sustains while mating with your physical, not less exquisite, appetites.

In the name of your version of human rights;

You cannot change the words of the refugees. You cannot "neutralize" them by turning the voice down according to your hearing skills. This is taking an action against a voice.

We had a very romantic break up. We went to Princes Islands to break up amid the sea and the beautiful swarms of hungry birds. It was a beautiful encounter, but not strong enough to last.

You do not love me enough.

Neither do I.

Next!

What comes next is a making of time. It is making it with other meaningful single times until the next beautiful encounter. It is a reduction of time from two to one sharing most of the time be it day or night. I feel the temperature in my head. It should be the sense of loss of two people good time and bad time together since it is part of it. Everything comes in twos in life. Weigh the positives and negatives and make peace with it. Peace is the closure in one and two. Peace is maintaining a positive energy after the change of the form of the encounter of two.

I miss your presence. You left me for two days with all of this load of us time. It is the beginning of the coping process. I have the room to myself and I am making a single time in it. It is painful! You know I have a lot of dignity and pride. I am not going to tell you I miss you. I do not know the use of telling since we decided to break up the two into one.

I am holding myself from meddling with the things you left behind. I smelt your jumper yesterday, and I know I should not do it again.

I changed.

I allow myself to cry whenever it is there. I lost you! Damn it!

We cannot change how we feel about each other. You say we lacked something, but we are lacking as human beings, we pursue lack in everything. It hurts that I could not give you that. I will make peace with it! I will make time with it!

My love was an ocean
it turned into a drop of water
and evaporated back to its source.

In Turkey, there is a tradition of pigeon feeding. Some take it as a profession. A lot of pigeon feeders are elderly people. When I feel like I am crumbling in life, I seek old people here. To me, they are the ones who made it in life, so they know best how to handle it.

I sneak up and sit beside her. She hands me one of the glasses of grain and says, "it is one lira. I lost my son two years ago, and I still cry. He died in an accident." She cries a bit. This is it!

She lost her son and she is living out in the world talking to people and enjoying the spring sun in Koca Mustafa Paşa square.

Another old woman sits on the next bench and she sells the pigeons' food too. The woman I am talking to starts competing with her for a customer. She says, "Does anyone sell their bread?" and I think to myself, "Does anyone sell their lover!"

She is 76 and sitting there competing with her pigeon feeding neighbour over work. I am 28 and I will compete to get my life back. Well, and bread too!

Everything makes it difficult to cope. The war has been going on for more than two years now. I feel like I am carrying my legs, that much effort it is to walk nowadays. The struggle to maintain life within that is.

When I was a child of 4 or 5 years, I had a dream. I wanted to grow up just to be able to turn the light on and off. Here I am almost 28 years, and for the first time I feel like I can turn the light on and off with you.

I played an Alawite folk song because of the energy in Alawite folk songs. It is 12 in the afternoon. I am energizing myself for the day. I want to have my coffee. I need one or two coffees to start the engine. I hear a light tap on the front door, and I open it to suddenly find you before me! I think to myself, "I will never see you again!

It is all my insecurity with myself that I cannot maintain a relationship and I throw it back in your face just like I did with my numerous exes.

My heart shrinks at the sight of you. I program myself when I break up. I become in control because I know the pain and the process very well.

We talk and you cry. I cannot believe you want to try with me again. My heart sinks for I am afraid of that which I cannot control; being in a relationship.

Yes, it feels like I am growing up to turn the light on and off.

I usually feel like I can grab people's core with one or two words like I can see what they are about. With you, it's different.

You are behind a thick glass as if you know you are so precious that you want to hide from the world.

We walk down from boulevard café in Taksim which I call the Syrian republic because it became a gathering place for Syrians who fled the land of war. I see hope in the Syrians gathering in it because they come from all cities and sects, but share a homeland and an experience of being in that land.

"Do you want to hold my hand here?"

I want a home where I can be myself, too!

Holding hands, we go down the alleyway leading to Istiklal Caddesi where a black dog occupies a certain spot. I tell you, "see, he will always be there just like Damascus." You don't like the comparison, but the way the dog occupies the space without even moving or caring about the passers-by is just like Damascus. Damascus doesn't care, it is like time. It will always be there!

Why is it cruel to smash a cockroach, or enjoy cutting a cat's tail?
I have seen more cruelty!
I have seen a cat thrown from the fourth floor by a girl of fifteen,
And I cried my heart out seeing it die!
I was four years old, I didn't know what cruelty is!

But I got used to cruelty! I live with it!
I breathe it in my own home!
I call it home,
One needs to have a home,
One needs to belong,
One breathes cruelty where minds are suffocated,
One sees cruelty, and turns blind,
One feels cruelty, and is numbed,
One smells cruelty, and gets addicted,
One touches cruelty, and deliciously makes love to it,
For making love to cruelty is an art in my home,
They French-kiss in my home,
They French-kiss passionately and twist tongues,
They cut tongues too!
They like to caress fine curved necks and suck on them till the blood dries out!
They massage backs in my home, and extremely enjoy breaking the spinal cord,
It's hot!

They fuck in my home, they fuck!
And they fuck hard!
they come!
They come out children of cruelty!
To crush cockroaches, and chase cats.
We are the children of cruelty,
We are the children of the fucking-hard in the darkness,
We are cut tongues and sucked necks,
We are broken spinal cords,
We have a home,
We belong!

I have been stuck in a graduate program for 7 months or more now. I want to feel miserable and be miserable. I decided to let myself be. There is a video of an Arab idol singer from Aleppo circulating on Facebook. The guy was singing a mawal[8] on Syria. It made me cry. What? As if I haven't been crying enough? A good song will always make you cry especially when the pain is immense and vivid. I go through the audition videos.

In one of the auditions, a beautiful woman comes out in front of the committee with a guy. They are from Iraq. The guy came with her to translate. She is Kurdish, but able to sing in Arabic although she doesn't understand the lyrics. She is from the north of Iraq, from Kurdistan. I thought how courageous and amazing she is; breaking this hegemony of Arabic in a land inhabited by several other ethnicities. In the following episode, she sings a beautiful traditional eastern makamat[9] song in Kurdish in Beirut. It was beautiful and the audience received it well.

She brought the Kurdish musical map and the Arab musical map very close with her presence in

---

[8] Mawal is a folk song and a traditional style of singing.

[9] A set of related musical notes based on a particular note forming the basis of a piece of music.

the program. Have they ever been that distant? Cultural exchange is inevitable between different social groups sharing one land. Kurds are not victims. They are survivors in their culture and legacy. Arab nationalism was and will always be a major failure. It just made other non-Arabs feel like they are strangers. Kurdish music is like our dream of a homeland where we can live and be ourselves, practitioners of our existence in a world free from tyranny and oppression. I disown my Arabism every time I listen to the call and yearning for a homeland in Kurdish music - a theme always present in their music. The times have changed. An Arab identity is no longer functional. Islamism is more appealing for homelands where majorities are oppressed Muslims regardless of their ethnicities.

"They" would organize pilgrimage in Mecca and sell Petroleum in Ahmadi."

I am supposed to give you a round of applause for such
a novel sarcastic observation! Or at least force myself to smile!
get over it,
I am sitting here! Talk to me!

Do you know where I come from? Do you know where I am heading?
You are so stuck in your history to look forward, to address the current realities.
Don't give me dates,
I know what happened in 1948,
I know what happened in 1947.
I know what happened in 1967.
I know what happened in 1970.
I know what happened in 1973.
I know what happened in 2009.

Damn it!
I can assure you I am not crushed yet!
But you are!
You are a lefty blind backward miserable dead
1948, 1947, 1967, 1970, 1973, 2009,

however, I like your "modernity" overlooking me,
You just don't tackle a whole culture

A whole strata
with a fine Cuban cigar,
I don't care where you got your tie from,
Or how much of a refined cultured asshole you look like!
Don't write me critical books and give me big words!

Let's get to the bottom of it!
Don't marginalize an Islamic readership by 'logical 14th Renaissance' like reading,
No wonder, there is Taliban!

You just don't get it with your big terminology,
People don't need PhD talks, excuse my fine ass!
And talking about readership, talking about politics,
talking about an elitist change,
I don't buy your bullshit!

You sit there, a god of your time, a god of knowledge,
Sipping your water with your stubborn preaching lips,
Look at me!
take my photos!
you need people like me!
I am coming! I am 1789!

Let us go into the night unrivaled by evil
Let us go into the tombs unrivaled by mortality
Let us go into loneliness unrivaled by the painful noise
Let us go into the nakedness unrivaled by the
enforced shrouds
Let us go bravely, proudly into our enchanting death
The death of the Free

"Thank God for your safety!"

"May God keep you safe too!"

"I will be so angry with you if you go to university again! I was dead scared!"

"I will go, again."

"Shut up! You are not going there again."

"Actually, this is what they want, and I want to learn regardless of mother nature itself."

I quote a verse from the Quran to him, don't throw yourself to destruction.

"It is shitty in Damascus and what happened today made me more determined to go to university. Fuck them! If you would just see how a girl was carrying her cheek in her hand."

Damn it! Fuck it!

"How is your psyche?"

I had this conversation with my nephew after a mortar rocket hit the architecture department at Damascus University. He was shocked and he wants to keep going to university to face the imperial powers playing with our life like chess pieces, wanting to break us. Life has changed. I do not know how is it now to be back there.

The last time I was in Syria was in 2011. Such a weird date! it has been two years and I do not think I have had any concept of how I spent my time there except for the many hours I spent every day on Facebook, the virtual home. It is no less catastrophic to try to belong in a virtual space; it is a delusional outlet; a preservation of being or escaping the reality on the ground. This is one of the greatest changes I have not been able to cope with so far. Making time or enjoying time was always an idea that resided there, Syria, at home.

I am just abroad on a mission to do something for home. Now, everything is shaken. I guess I am starting to accept it and embrace it to find a way to rethink of my ideas of home and how I relate to it. Something is broken; the country is changed, destroyed. I am not scared for the future of Syria. It survived a lot throughout its history. What I am scared of is more death and destruction.

Otherwise,
There is no otherwise,
It is who we are.
Like silence
lined up in mute patterns,
constant
in our timeless agony
and longing for an
everlasting change
an exit where there is no return,
where silence is peace
and muteness is a language.

Hope is life, and waiting is life. Waiting means you are anticipating and expecting something to come and change and hence you are living, you did not give up. To recapture the decision of your life and what to do with it as an oppressed Syrian in the world did not prove to be just difficult, but a complete human disaster. Which is more important: the principle or the soul? Obviously, the principle and a better life was more important than what existed before, a life with no dignity.

So, for dignity and a better life we die now, for the coming Syrians to live better with dignity and choice over their destinies. Home is not a hotel you leave when things get bad. She is living there now! And me, I am having a psychological crisis and allowing myself to be weak and human as one special friend told me.

My friend came to visit yesterday. I consider him my sibling in Istanbul. He said time is passing, and this is your life passing too. Whether in pain, pleasure or peace, it is passing. He is right. What did I make in those two years? Feeling guilt and pain for the loss is not going to change anything. I am here and there; split in two time zones. And here I am afraid to go outside my place and reconnect with the world around me as if I have fallen into some sort of a gap in time, or a change in psyche and time-space relevance. Why does it matter this much? There are Syrians in far worse situations, but pain is pain, that is my conclusion. Hitting the bottom is rising anew, different, and changed. War is also an aspect of our life as humans.

My brother, Ahmet told me yesterday he used to listen to George Wassouf songs when it would rain in winter until he fell asleep in his room in Aleppo. It was very tense the way he said it. He never spoke of his feelings.

"Do you miss Syria?" I said.

"Syria is not ours anymore. It is for those who are living in it regardless of the immense difficulty of life under war."

Life is passing.

I live here in a big room in an old area in the huge cosmopolitan city of Istanbul. I am physically here and I am a human being who has a memory card in the universe. I have made home a divine place to keep me grounded. Home, the load of memory, oppression, freedom, bravery, war, and humanity at its best. I am home since I am the memory. I create it myself and place it. I grab it and unfold it until I become in harmony with the universe.

Life is passing. To observe anew, we need new eyes. To live anew, we need new senses. I am one of those millions in the city with a story. Life is one and is beautiful even when it is harsh and catastrophic. To walk and look around watching them walking, going on with their life is beautiful. A woman at the corner puts out her corn to sell to strangers and exchange a few conversations. What a beautiful sight! And I come home to write about how beautiful life is if we change how we look at it. Our brains need breaks from thoughts and ideas. They need a 10 minutes' connection with layered clouds in a blue sky on an autumn day. There is something about September and its smell, a revival. Life is seasoned and we are seasoned.

I am hungry for life that I wanted to scream while walking among my fellow humans, live it for its passing. As if I want to announce my self-discovery or a friend's wisdom to the crowd.

In Arabic, there is a word that is pronounced kaynuneh; the verb "kin" means to settle. "Kaynuneh" means to get warm and homey during winter or to settle. Settlement can be physical or spiritual. Some call it emotional security. I think of it like ants hiding under ground in winter. Humans rest at home. I wash the dishes and come to find you all cosy and warm under the dark purple sheets you brought today. I do my prayers and you are reading with your glasses on and I am thinking of my kaynuneh with you. One of the greatest things in life is to feel home with someone, and I do with you.

I am trying to consult my Syria within me. The Syria I grew up in, the Syria I love and is in pain and uncertainty. Syria's uncertainty is mine even if I am building a life somewhere else. Our existence is like molecules encompassing all time-space memories. It is in the air regardless of the current niche. My life is with you. I am watching the Magnificent Century[10] series, and it got to me the way humans grow evil when they become powerful. I come to bed late around four and you are sleeping. I come slowly, and you, asleep, smile at me and turn around for me to hold you. It is peace. You are my lodge. There is an Ayah in Quran that says Allah has created, from your souls, husbands and wives so you can take lodge into them.

Yesterday, I had a small panic attack on the bus. It felt like my lungs were suffocating, I had music in my ears. I got off the bus and started walking and smoking. I got off in Haseki area before Aksaray and walked to Beyazıt where my university is. The cold wind massaged my cheeks and my thoughts; rough and sweet wind. I pass through Aksaray and a guy followed me. He knew I am Arab and possibly Syrian from the way we

---

[10] Muhteşem Yüzyıl, a Turkish TV series.

wear our veils. He is from Aleppo and lived in Greece for the last 10 years.

"It is my first time in Turkey in 10 years," he said.

I asked him, "What do you do? Trade like the Aleppians?"

"Yes, trade of humans," he replied, mockingly.

Aksaray maybe is and has always been a transitional area for migrants from within and outside Turkey. I love the area though, lots of stories. . . It feels like the hope and the shit of the world at the same time. It is old, I love old neighbourhoods. They touch me. Perhaps, I need to open up more to the new, the modern or whatever this general trend in the world is. The panic attack shook me a bit. I think it is a reminder again not to stress and take things slowly. I need to learn how to let my feelings be when I feel them instead of my psyche reminding me every now and then.

Perhaps since I have an insatiable attitude to life and living, I started to direct it outward more than towards my own inward beauty. The wind in winter is cold and strong. It is gentle, too. I went down to the rocks this time, and sat singing to the waves. I sang to them in Arabic and Turkish. I sang to them in a high voice and enjoyed the freedom of doing it. I am just like you, in need of an infinite space to realize the potential of my energy. I woke up drunk today. Drunk with the dream I had, and the overdose of my thoughts. I had you naked on the sofa in the guest room in my family's old apartment. The setting is a bit unusual for making love to you, but it is the setting of all my dreams for some reason. How can you love two people at the same time without feeling guilty? You come to me in dreams and on the phone and I just respond because I cannot see the end or the objective of voicing it. However, it is like an extra dose of energy filling me all over, or adding to what is called me. Everyone has different energies and I am wondering if two energies melted into each other, why would they give this beautiful feeling? It’s a stupid question and I do not call it love. People call it love to simplify it. I, liking to philosophize about feelings, would rather call it pure beauty from a beautiful source of the universe. It does not hurt and if it does, it does not hate. It diminishes borders and sets free for the sake of its realization.

While trying to sleep, I think to myself, relationship boundaries are like nation-state boundaries.

I need to survive the exquisite smell of rain on the barren streets. It is too beautiful to last! And I do survive mapping out the silence in clusters of letters, believing that my unreturned quests are the core of my creative despair, which I need to last. I survive your hands reaching out to me by putting off the fire in my knees. I squeeze my heart between my feet and knock it over your sentences in a small talk. I need to survive your longing eyes to find truth in mine because truth is scary, and is not affordable most of the time.

I leave because it is easier to crush my soul, it is familiar. I do it to myself all the time. You see how I survive the influx of passion putting on masks and summoning all kinds of phobias. But here, I am powerful. No one can defeat me or gain grip over my heart!

I am pregnant. The grown-up child in my mind is giving birth to something. Language is in labour and it has strangled me. My lungs and my throat are contracting. The air is a streaming chaos of existence which we call creativity. The creation of an expression. The inhalation and exhalation of being to entertain the "being." I can see a child smelling like white jasmine and hesitant to come into "being".

The thought of you is like thinking of my heaven. The close and distant road to redemption. In my worst times, I remember you calming my soul after a panic attack. I was in your room lying on the bed while the cold breeze caressed my weary soul and my face was on your chest. At peace, there on your chest where my heaven is. Close and distant just like being in the world. You were discussing philosophy and academia with my ex-best friend. I could hear your discussion, the two of you, in my ears, but I preferred the heaven of your chest over all the learning and lessons of institutions.

Now, we had a long talk about the difficulties of our characters, being together, and the difficulties of facing and being together in the world. I feel troubled. The thought of losing you is suffocating, but the thought of committing to you and facing the world is just as suffocating. I turn 30 next year, and I think it's time to face my world with myself. It is all unsettling. Do I go back home? Do I settle with you in Istanbul? It is this indecisive emotional time, being pulled in so many directions that I prefer to go into an endless sleep. I love you and hate disturbing your most beautiful soul with my unsettling world, and I think you deserve better.

An elderly friend of the family told me her story and I think she must tell it to everyone. She spoke of a love she couldn't be with, and how she married someone else. She had a good life with him, but when she was widowed she spoke to her old love. Society and her children prohibited her from marrying him. I asked her do we ever forget the love we have with someone? Did you forget him while you were with your husband for 40 years? She said no, we still talk with the hasret[11] of bygone days and the happiness promised in them. I would live on the memories we have, I think. I could live on the memory of your soft skin while you hold me after I land. Yes, I believe, I could use this to give me peace when I need you. I landed to meet my heaven there in your soft arms.

[11] Hasret is Turkish for longing and melancholic desire.

I have received many guests from my home in Syria in my home in Istanbul. My brother, my brother in law, and my sisters' kids. Part of home came to me. It felt like too much, such a stressful and emotional time. I had made up my mind to settle in Istanbul and not go back there or watch the news. But home came to me with all its incomprehensive intensity; an intensity beyond human understanding.

A friend tells me, whoever comes from Syria is like a drowning man holding onto a stick and you are the stick. They will drown us with them. I thought a lot about it. This is my family but my relative wants me to carry the responsibility of him trying to build a new life away from home. I couldn't and I thought I was sinking in my life, so I exploded. They left back to a torn homeland. I felt too guilty to eat, and be with my love in the security and safety we were enjoying.

I thought afterwards how I didn't buy my nieces and nephews things to take with them. How I didn't show them their aunt's world in this country. Because in-between the horrible stories of home, on the verges and edges of life and death, I couldn't be just their aunt. Albeit, their aunt who couldn't hold up their father and who thought she was losing her life and her time. I became disgusted with myself as a human and humans in general and the world we built.

But is my friend's sentence true or the reality of our condition? I remember one of the neighbourhood cats slept on her dead kitten. Her life moved on and she brought more kittens into the world.

I am homesick my love. I miss my land and my memories, my parents and my siblings, my nieces and nephews, and my home. My parents are getting older. I have not been with them there for 3 years now. I am tired of this schizophrenia of being in the middle of two time-zones; two lives. I am tired of the double life I am leading, too.

So instead of deciphering this 500-year-old Ottoman compilation, of what seems to be an autobiography of an ambitious statesman who complained about how he never got what he wanted in life, I want to write. Write about the two days I spent watching a TV series filmed in the streets, spaces and everything I knew to be me for the past 27 years. Write how I express my homesickness to a place that will never be the same again. And maybe 500 years later, someone will read the stories of this God-forsaken geography and this particular war. So what? All stories are the same. Why call it a story? What makes it worthy of being written? Defying being

commonly human and mortal? Or the act of defying being human, mortal and fragile in a certain geography?
I befriended her several weeks ago, a friend suggested that we talk. She is a talented artist. I thought she was melodramatic, posting a lot of the news and grievances of Syria so I unfriended her. She died a few days ago, of a heart failure.

This fucking war has changed all of us. It's all the fucking stories of pain. My family, my beloved family they all have changed. When I get close, they shatter this little fucking paradise that I have in this corner of Istanbul. Stories of unsettlement, of the peace gone out of the gates of Syria to return God knows when and where. And I tell myself this will pass, peace will return and hence this little fake paradise of mine and theirs, and mine in theirs. I tell myself go away, run away to Europe, to another fake paradise. I tell myself go build another life far away with your beloved, so that my Syrian folk won't sweep my little paradise again.

Then I think of my brother who always refused to build his little paradise and I think to myself maybe he is the rebel among us. Who knows what happens when your mind's peace is swept by all this shit that comes to mind. I come running in panic to the bathroom sink in my little paradise to wash my face with cold water to remind myself of the absurdity of it all. And because it's fake I don't take it too seriously, I laugh at the mirror, my little venting paradise.

She tells me, you overestimate your feelings and you get involved in your thoughts too much. But what else can I do when I am at the intersections of peace and war, my family and my life, and the fucking degree I am trying to finish to make something of myself in the absurdity of it all.

It is not absurd. There is much peace in the face of a cat demanding love and food.

It is time to close the curtains. The memory is full. The defensive psyche is at its best. Picking and giving up stories. A Sufi traveller: estranged of all times, takes nothing of the past except for his faith, roaming the cities and people. Those who have less faith, await hope and closures, travel with heavy chaotic things. The voice of survival is often absent but pops up on necessary calls of nature. Fight or die! Die before you die! We will put a tombstone on your bed. Beds can turn into tombs. Would you ever make peace with exile and oppression? Spin twelve times until they disappear and you breathe yourself anew.

What are we afraid of? The unknown, the loss, or the anticipation that although it's really shitty now it is still better than with no one around. Maybe this is it? This is the bottom line. I feel so frustrated every time this happens. What is the use of opening up and saying you miss someone when they want you to explain their feelings instead of actually feeling your feelings and saying a few nice things out of love to relieve you, is it this big a deal? I mean seriously?! And it feels so stupid to say it.

Niyaz moved between different space- time zones. It was her drive to know more and live more of herself and of life. It was easier to envision movement and adaptation in the different space-time zones when the anchor was perfectly rested in Syria. The anchor is the grounding space-time zone. The anchor is the grounding memory. When the anchor became uncertain, her life became uncertain, and movement between different space-time zones becomes more difficult. The difficulty is rather not adaptation nor drive. The difficulty is in recreating an anchor. Is it possible to create the anchor within herself? In so doing, regardless of movement and different space-time zones, the anchor rests within your body, memory, and soul. How is it possible to anchor a trans-spatial memory without falling back on waiting to recapture the first anchor?

Niyaz, like hundreds of thousands of Syrians, was forced into exile. In a neighbouring country, she rented a place. She made the effort to choose furniture, make a reflection of herself and her memories in the little space she had. Things became a burden. She got attached to her things. İsn't it funny? She thought to herself. We come without things into the world. Is this the message or a revelation of when you are exiled or on the move? That you should let go of things or not have them in the first place to make your movement easier. Syrians migrate to Europe, or wealthy countries in Europe, without things. Perhaps they carry their documents or mobile phones. It is either a thrill or a liberation to gamble on your life. It is either the promise, illusion, of a grounding existential security or an escape to normalcy. There, a breed of people have normal lives.

Tell us how you race with time in the streets, boulevards, cafes, shops, factories, and every work place in Istanbul to get a job? Tell us of the race with time to hold onto something against the waves taking everything from you. Tell us the story of your first agricultural attempts. Tell us how you fought against the waters to hold onto a land and plant your seeds. Tell us how hard it was to cultivate it. Under the stillness of waters at Galata bridge, there are swimmers in dark waters. It is too serene on the metro bridge crossing from Vezneciler to Şişhane.

I woke up with thoughts of your visit to my dream. You are only a possibility and that is what makes you different. Love when taken is no more a possibility, it is a reality shared and cherished. I woke up with a possibility in my heart. On most days, I wake up with a possibility in my mind. I force it. Today, I sipped my strong-cardamom coffee, content. I felt the awakening caffeine in my head. I wonder if it is the sunshine or the possibility creeping into my heart that made me so content. When the struggle for life is existential, you are cornered with concepts and images of security; ultimately, material security. You struggle to live, and your dreams are evaporating. Is spirituality a luxury in times of lack of existential security? Is your visit to my dream and the possibility of the heart a mere unconscious escape to feel other realities? I should say imagination and escape are also at times a reality we choose to create.

I sat with a 3-lira cup of Nescafe opposite Aya Sofia in the sunshine listening to folk music and looking through our archive of possibilities: moments where we were happy or drinking the nectar of good company, just the sort of company of one nodding and the other understanding.

You either live here or there. At least, try to live here. "Memories are insidious bastards," one of my love's brilliant sentences. I tell my nephew do not get immersed in stories of the war from our city. It takes from your energy and focus here. In exile, you can barely push yourself to find some ground and keep it. Check up on your family. This is all you need to know here and now. I felt like reading Surat Lokman to him. Perhaps I felt like Lokman giving advice on how to live in exile during war where family and memory are at war. In exile, we race against time.

Each state gets a bite of our flesh in exchange for our soul, even the devil gets a bite. Yusufpaşa, a central neighbourhood in Istanbul and big transport node buzzes with the signs of Arabic restaurants and cafes. A hundred years after the fall of the Ottoman empire, Arabic script finds its way back to Istanbul, another Fateh[12] it is. This time of food, cardamom filled coffee, and Syrian flat bread.

[12] Fateh - Arabic and Turkish meaning conquest.

A silent geography

There is not enough evil
to quench my thirst!
I can even go further kissing
sadistically,
a kiss where I suck on the blood of your lips
and watch how it hurts,
or I might excavate your armpits,
crack your facial bones,
lusciously observe the process of my insatiable hunger
to deform you;
a passionate kiss again where I suck on you
dehydrated body on the cross,
and crucify you once more,
till my kisses tear open
dark spots in your body.
When I finish my mapping
I shall hang you up
A silent geography,
for I am no Heathcliff,
but I may be another Bronte.

"Will I ever return home?" she asked.

"I do not know, but you are going to return," the other responded.

"Maybe when I am 40, how can you be so certain?" she asked again.

"I have faith and you will return before you turn 40."

"But explain to me how do you know? How can you have faith in that?" she asked again.

"I have faith maybe because I need to!" came the response.

"I wish I can have that faith in return," she thought silently. She thought of how she wants her parents to be alive when she returns, or otherwise, can you call a return to a new reality a return?

How can one simply accept the Syrian tragedy without questioning faith, God and justice? The only answer that we found is that we somehow deserved this. But there are innocent people and children! How can we digest this and go on with our spiritual life intact? I am very angry at the world and at God. Less so now because I am trying to keep my faith. One needs to have faith. Faith breeds faith. Losing one's faith in something that affects our other forms of faith: faith in the human race, faith in one's self, or faith in nature. I love God so much that I became so angry. I have not lost my faith. It changed. I do not have the answer to the Syrian tragedy or to my own tragedy. How do I blend in the two things? Faith and tragedy?

These times are not human-friendly and I spend half of my life reuniting with you to counter the times.

It is black blank bleak,
disentangle yourself and mine,

I will dance you dervish on the
tips of my fingers,
I know you can come to the land of light,
with me!

Take off your attire, revolve round
me!

I do not need your love, neither your yearning!
I only need your wounds, and your agony!

There is no leave-taking! The room was all lightness. The shutters quite closed and the window wide open. A current of undisturbed fresh air gently pushes through the shutters to find its course to the open pages interrupting a fair humane silence. Two shapes were eyeing each other with a full resignation to the calm yet passionate atmosphere of the dimly lit room. In the lingering process of love, a cigarette being smoked mingling with a very distinguished perfume.

The pent-up fear unleashed, strangely extended the limited space of the room. It momentarily felt like Eden. It was perfect, complete, and no such satisfaction. An untimely sun rise, and you fled away. The room shrank to its earthly size and the air kept in without the window. The very distinguished perfume imprisoned my sense and I slept under the blue sheets thinking, “it was but a dream within a dream.”

It has been the landscape, the song, the pain, the joy, and the contradiction of life twisting quests and creeds. A sweeping calamity when life seemed idealistically static and balanced. It spread wide open like a whirlwind taking me in.

Revolving around you like ritual or a gravity. It all just turned a mere depravity.

We didn't sink down yet
And we might
The scary abyss below us
Full of mystery
Didn't sweep us yet
But we can surly admit
We have fallen apart

Our courses are indefinite and obscure
But we can rise up
Not together
But apart.

And chilling, I let go of the ant, gather all my sides, and move on....

The water fountain is but another recess,
Crystal clear showers in vicious circles.
On my right side, a red scholarly bag carrying pieces of me;
On my left side, my cup of coffee, my cigarettes and my time!
I have always waited the one day when I will have them all on one side.

In the middle there is an ant that thunders my ease,
and blows my determination.
it gracefully courses my leg,
renders me to the level of envy!
Perhaps it has a similar name, and
even better;
Its name doesn't mean frog in Spanish!
It will gather her life in a warm winter, and winter only rekindles my chilliness!
And chilling, I let go of the ant, gather all my sides, and move on....
We offer death the remnants of selfishness in survival,
We become sadists for sacrifice,
And death, you might want to run away
because from now on, you are wanted!

Too much mortality around you that if I get the flu, I worry I am dying. Our life is very cheap on the scale of nations. But every nation is getting its sum of our soul as it humps the back of refugees. NGOs flourish their feast upon the dead Syrian body. Parasites everywhere and I think to myself, the best answer to these parasites is to let them think they have you and get the most off them.

Enjoying life is the answer to all this hatred and the vengeful world of our mortal bodies. Our soul is free as the wind driving the boats to Europe. Free as the bargain and gamble on life on the waters of the Mediterranean, and the cost of the journeys of the free on all borders. Now we are everywhere, we expanded our existence living or dead on all continents. Putting your anger into a good path means waking up and enjoying your Syrian coffee and your cigarettes. Being visible where you are not wanted. Saying hello to a racist woman preaching about loving animals but hating Syrians.

The answer is in enjoying the streets of Istanbul regardless of transit and human withdrawal of their past.

I lost a piece of my heart and my soul with you. I buried the piece in the grave yard stretching from Yedikule to Edirnekapı where trees sustain the lives of the dead Istanbulites.

Give love to love; love belongs to love. Remember in the times of roaming mortality on land and sea to take a bite of my apple when you let go of your fears. Scared humans are not alive; they inhibited their souls in the realm of the dead. Is it not funny that fear is supposed to help us survive, but it can make us stop living?! Is there a more dangerous threat than living, feeling alive, feeling full of life? Remember to keep the lines clear so you can have a piece of my apple and a cup of my coffee. Cutting someone off from your life is an aggressive, cold and hurtful act. Remember to account for its consequence with your rotten apple and cold coffee.

I will grab your hand
like the cardamom grabs the air in the room
while making fresh coffee,
and will sneak into your spine
like the steam evaporating from the cup
this is how I will taste in your ears
the belonging mania!

I am not angry anymore, I understand. Life brings people in and out. Sometimes people's presence become unbearable especially when too many unsolved issues hover over their heads as they converse and continue to wear their social uniforms. But if I do not see you at your most vulnerable, if I do not see you cry or feel insecure, how can we possibly bond and be friends?

And if only playing the drums can match
The beats of the veins on the necklines,
And if only the colorful ornaments on the head
are fire and water in the lungs breathing over the window.
Shy is the music of the senses, concealed in the noise.

It's exotic that you think I am exotic.
Here in this apartment in Galata, the land of foreigners, hippies, drunkards, transit migrants, white Turks, working class Kurds, drug dealers and Gulf tourists, I will take you. I will be your migrant. I will be your third world smartass. Your lover on the move. And you will be the land of my dreams and hopes. You will be my resettlement to the land of secularism, individualism, human rights and great values. I kiss you angrily and with each kiss you fall more in love with my interesting other and I fall in love with your great civilized other.

I pushed you to the edge of my pain
Sucking it in-between your ribs,
Capturing your breath and the rhythm of fingers;
Stretching,
Contracting.
I lined up my manias on your limbs
Pressing your knees,
Holding your feet,

I measured my chaos against your neckline
And unleashed it in the trembles of your ears,

Do not close your eyes,
Keep my insanity intact!

Loving you is like dying without leaving a legacy.
It is the absence of my presence and the sterility of
my fertility.
You are the gravity pulling me onto the collapsing
sphere,
Cannot you see how ugly you are?

Black tea, mint and jazz

Is that mint, sweetheart?
Your fresh intoxicating mint,
Is that your cup of heavy black tea?
Brought in a hot afternoon,
while jazz is played loudly and slowly
like the drops of sweat on my forehead

If there should be a day
where I would feel sober drinking black tea with fresh mint.
If there would be a day
while I would sit in a hot afternoon,
listening to jazz played loudly and slowly
without stretching unknown and obscured,
sweetened and vulnerable,
not unhappy, not exactly intoxicated,
but fixed sweetheart,
fixed in your black tea
your fresh mint,
your jazz,
Loudly,
Slowly,
Silently.

Your taste still mesmerizes my mind like some cinnamon in a fresh tea. Your taste can still hypnotize me like the bloodshed of my countrymen, that excessive pain!

To miss someone who is absent is a normal feeling, but when you keep missing them, and you know there is little possibility that you will see them, the missing turns into a longing and then into a burden. You start forgetting the little details of their presence, how they carry themselves, how they talk, what their hands looked like. The last time I left Syria, I made sure to map my father's and mother's hand in my mind. I still remember their hands very well. I am grateful for that.

My mother visited me in Istanbul two years ago. The day before she left I took her to my favourite café in Istanbul. The café, called Yunus Emre, overlooks the Haliç and the beautiful lights of Istanbul. I was introduced to my special friend there and in that very same café, we stayed until 3 in the morning getting to know each other.

I sat there with my mother in June. The air was so full of summer life. She missed my father and home by that point and could not wait to go back. All the time we were sipping our coffee, we could not talk properly knowing we do not know when we will meet next and with the possibility that we might not meet at all looming in the background. I was choking on my thoughts and feelings. I remember all the condensed feelings in my chest, almost suffocating me, but I had to pull myself together and wear the 'I am fine face' before her so she would not worry. A few tears escaped our eyes in the café, that much we could not control after all.

I went to that café three months later with a couple of friends, and that was the last time I ever went there. The friends I did not like much at the time, and I had a panic attack with all those condensed feelings. I never went back there again.

At home, we were raised to conceal our feelings, all kinds of feelings. We become embarrassed if we cry or show love or any other form of affection. It is awkward even though I am blessed with a loving family and home. Things changed during the war years. At first, war took its toll on us and we did not communicate much. As my sister said, your memory becomes locked and you live in oblivion while you are in Syria. As time passed and there was no sign of the war stopping, we started communicating better. Now, we show our love over WhatsApp, Facebook, Line and Skype. However, we hide our anxiety and worry. It does not get anyone anywhere.

My dad bought himself a tablet to connect with everyone abroad and to live through it as life tightens in Syria. It is nice to live somewhere else even virtually.

He called us via Line one evening and we had a three-hour singing session. The songs ranged from classic Oum Kalthoom and Fairuz to modern ones like George Wassouf. Everyone sang except my mother. She ran away from the emotional setting. My father is known in the family for inventing mawals and he sang one about us, the ones, in exile. It was hard to feel that much emotion. We cried all of us. I came back and sang to him and we cried again. Showing love and care to loved ones is a good thing that came out of the war since the possibility of loss is higher, and absences are longer.

A friend of mine who carries the burden of Syria on his shoulder tells me he is afraid that Syrians are forgetting Syria. I tell him we want to forget; otherwise how do you live with carrying so much on your back. So much on your back slows your walking until you stop, and if you want to walk, you have to let go of your burdens, even longings. Simply because one day this whole thing will be over, and we will have what we want. This, like all things in life will pass and we have got to live while alive.

I let go of my anger, but not my bitterness at the world. I let go because living is a gift, surviving is a gift. Freedom is only the gift of the dead. When the world is against you; turn back to your close world and cherish it. And I will go back to my favourite café in Istanbul to cherish the memory and the good times I spent with my mother. To quote one of my brother's amazing sentences, "there are memories for which we can live more than a life time."

The "thing" is in the rectangle of the sprinkling sun-rays on the surface of water. It is in the invisible beauty of the vanishing lights. The "thing" is in two pairs of shoes on a bench observing existence. It is in the immersed forgetfulness in being; in facing unfathomed waters! And "everything" behind the bench is rather silently troubled in the air. "Everything" thickens painlessly behind the bench strangled by beauty borders. The "thing" is "everything" suspended in overwhelming waters and unreachable air. The "thing" is "everything" warmed by sprinkling sun-rays on the surface of waters in the relaxing state of unification with existence unfathomed, unpredicted, and infinite. The "thing" is "everything" surrendering to beauty borders uncrossed by answers and knowledge. The "thing" is "everything" between waters and air, sun and light, a bench and shoes. It is an existence untroubled by questions, but troubled by interpretations.

Rana Abdul Fattah - Biography

Rana Abdul Fattah, a lover of Istanbul, cats and coffee, grew up in Damascus suburb in Syria. She studied English literature in Damascus and the USA. She came to Istanbul to study and due to the war in Syria remained in the city. She previously published a book of poetry in Syria. Some of those poems are included in this book.

Palewell Press

Palewell Press is an independent publisher based in London, handling poetry, fiction and non-fiction with a focus on human rights, social history and the environment. The Editor may be reached at enquiries@palewellpress.co.uk

www.ingramcontent.com/pod-product-compliance
Ingram Content Group UK Ltd.
Pitfield, Milton Keynes, MK11 3LW, UK
UKHW020238250726
13967UKWH00001B/432

9 780995 535121